F
DESTINATION

THE HORROR LEGACY

ALEXIS I THOMPSON

All rights reserved. No part of this book may be reproduced, distributed, or transmitted in any form or by any means, including photocopying, recording, or other electronic or mechanical methods, without the prior written permission of the copyright owner except in the case of brief quotations embodied in critical reviews and certain other noncommercial uses permitted by copyright.

Copyright © 2025 by Alexis I. Thompson

Table of Contents

Introduction.. 3

Chapter 1
The Evolution of the Final Destination Franchise................................ 6

Chapter 2
Death as a Villain: The Ultimate Slasher Without a Face........................10

Chapter 3
Generational Curses and Horror's Obsession with Bloodlines...................14

Chapter 4
Tony Todd: A Horror Icon's Legacy..... 18

Chapter 5
The Anatomy of a Perfect Horror Death Scene................................... 21

Chapter 6
Horror's Future: What Final Destination: Bloodlines Means for the Genre................................... 25

Conclusion...29

Introduction

Horror has always thrived on inevitability. From the doomed teens of *Friday the 13th* to the lurking shadows of *Halloween*, audiences have long been drawn to the inescapable grasp of fate. But no franchise has captured the sheer unpredictability of death quite like *Final Destination*. Unlike traditional horror films where a masked killer or supernatural entity hunts victims, *Final Destination* turns death itself into the antagonist—unseen, unstoppable, and relentless. It's not a matter of *if* someone will die, but *how*.

Now, over a decade since the last installment, *Final Destination: Bloodlines* breathes new life into the series, taking its premise in a fresh direction while staying true to its core appeal: elaborate, brutal, and eerily plausible deaths. More than just another horror sequel, *Bloodlines* taps into something deeper—our collective fear of fate and the unnerving idea that death is always watching.

But why does *Final Destination* still resonate with audiences after all these years? The answer lies in its unique approach to horror. Unlike slasher films, where characters can theoretically escape the killer, *Final Destination* leaves no room for survival. Once you're on Death's list, it's only a matter of time. This unavoidable doom creates a different kind of tension—one that lingers long after the credits roll.

The franchise also excels in making everyday life terrifying. It turns ordinary, mundane situations—like driving behind a logging truck, using a tanning bed, or boarding a roller coaster—into moments of impending doom. By preying on real-world fears, *Final Destination* keeps viewers looking over their shoulders, making it one of the few horror franchises that truly alters how people perceive their surroundings.

Bloodlines takes this fear and amplifies it through its generational curse storyline. By linking death's vengeance to past actions, the film explores the idea that fate is not just personal but hereditary. The sins of the past don't just haunt the guilty—they extend to their descendants, making death's grip even tighter.

As horror continues to evolve, *Final Destination* proves that some fears never fade. The thought of a faceless force, waiting for the perfect moment to strike, will always unnerve us. And with *Bloodlines*, death is back—more inventive, more brutal, and more inevitable than ever.

Chapter 1

The Evolution of the *Final Destination* Franchise

When *Final Destination* debuted in 2000, it offered something entirely new to the horror genre. At a time when slasher films dominated theaters, this movie broke the mold. There was no masked killer lurking in the shadows, no vengeful ghost haunting an old house—just death itself, operating through an intricate series of chain reactions. The film's success paved the way for a franchise that would span over two decades, each installment refining and escalating the formula that made the original so terrifying.

At its core, *Final Destination* was a simple but brilliant concept: a group of people narrowly avoids a massive catastrophe, only to realize they were never meant to survive. One by one, they are killed off in bizarre, elaborate accidents, as though the universe itself is correcting an error. Unlike other horror movies where characters might fight back against a tangible threat, *Final Destination* made survival impossible. No matter what they did, death found a way.

The sequel, *Final Destination 2* (2003), took everything that worked in the first film and dialed it up. The infamous highway pileup scene remains one of the most terrifying and realistic horror openings ever put to film. This movie also introduced the idea that people could manipulate Death's design—at least temporarily—by bringing new life into the world.

Final Destination 3 (2006) leaned into the spectacle, with an opening disaster set on a roller coaster and a greater focus on gruesome, almost sadistic deaths. It was also the first film in the franchise to introduce the idea that clues about upcoming deaths could be hidden in photographs.

By the time *The Final Destination* (2009) arrived, the franchise was at risk of becoming repetitive. Though it featured impressive 3D effects, many critics and fans considered it weaker than its predecessors. But then came *Final Destination 5* (2011), which revitalized the series with a clever twist—revealing in its final moments that it was actually a prequel to the first film, tying the timeline together in a shocking way.

Now, over a decade later, *Final Destination: Bloodlines* reinvents the franchise once again. By introducing a generational curse, it expands the mythology beyond individual accidents. This time, Death isn't just after one group—it's after an entire bloodline, making survival even more impossible.

Each film in the *Final Destination* series has built upon the last, proving that death never takes a break. And with *Bloodlines*, it's clear that the franchise still has plenty of life left—even as its characters continue to meet their gruesome ends.

Chapter 2

Death as a Villain: The Ultimate Slasher Without a Face

Horror is full of iconic killers—Michael Myers, Freddy Krueger, Jason Voorhees—but *Final Destination* took a radically different approach. Instead of a masked figure or supernatural entity hunting its victims, the franchise made Death itself the villain. There's no physical form, no personality, no voice—just an unstoppable force correcting what it sees as a mistake. This lack of a tangible antagonist makes Death one of the most terrifying villains in horror history.

Unlike traditional slashers, where characters have a chance to fight back, *Final Destination* strips them of that hope. Death is inevitable, and no amount of running, hiding, or planning will stop it. This makes the franchise unique because survival isn't about defeating the villain—it's about delaying the inevitable. Even the most careful, paranoid characters eventually fall victim to fate's relentless pull.

What sets Death apart from other horror villains is its creativity. Instead of using knives, chainsaws, or supernatural abilities, it orchestrates elaborate, Rube Goldberg-style death traps that turn everyday objects into lethal weapons. A simple cup of coffee spills, causing a series of events that end with a character being impaled, crushed, or incinerated. Fans of the franchise don't just fear Death—they fear the ordinary. The movies make people rethink everything, from standing under ceiling fans to driving behind a lumber truck.

This approach taps into a deep psychological fear: the idea that no matter how careful we are, we're never truly safe. *Final Destination* doesn't rely on jump scares—it builds dread by showing how small, insignificant actions can spiral into catastrophe. A loose screw, a forgotten turn of a wrench, or a gust of wind can be the difference between life and death. It forces viewers to imagine how easily their own lives could end in a freak accident.

Another reason Death works so well as a villain is its lack of emotion. Unlike Freddy or Jason, who have motivations rooted in revenge or sadism, Death is indifferent. It's not personal—it's just correcting the natural order. This makes it even scarier because there's no reasoning with it. It doesn't get angry, it doesn't make mistakes, and it never stops.

With *Final Destination: Bloodlines*, Death returns with a new angle—the idea that it can linger across generations. This raises the stakes beyond individual survival, suggesting that fate doesn't just claim one person at a time, but entire families. By expanding the mythology, *Bloodlines* reinforces the franchise's core message: you can't cheat Death forever.

Chapter 3

Generational Curses and Horror's Obsession with Bloodlines

Horror has always been fascinated with legacy—especially when it comes to curses. From haunted families to inescapable bloodlines, the idea that fate can pass from one generation to the next is a recurring theme in the genre. *Final Destination: Bloodlines* taps directly into this fear, introducing a terrifying twist: Death isn't just coming for those who cheated it—it's coming for their descendants, too.

The concept of a generational curse isn't new. Movies like *The Omen* (1976), *Hereditary* (2018), and even *Halloween* (1978) have explored the idea that some fates are passed down like an inherited disease. In *The Omen*, Damien isn't just a regular child—he's the Antichrist, burdened with a destiny he didn't choose. In *Hereditary*, a family is unknowingly tied to a dark supernatural force, leading to tragic consequences. And in *Halloween*, Laurie Strode spends decades being hunted by Michael Myers simply because she's part of his history.

What makes *Final Destination: Bloodlines* unique is how it applies this theme to fate itself. The grandmother's decision to save lives in the 1960s wasn't just an act of heroism—it was a mistake in Death's eyes. By interfering with the natural order, she unknowingly doomed her entire family. This shifts *Final Destination* from being about individual survival to being about a doomed lineage, making the horror even more suffocating.

The idea of inescapable fate is one of the most unsettling themes in horror. It takes away any illusion of control. No matter what the characters do, no matter how much they try to avoid it, Death will always find a way. In previous *Final Destination* films, characters could attempt to "cheat" Death by following its patterns and trying to disrupt them. But in *Bloodlines*, the scope is much larger—this isn't just about one person outsmarting Death. It's about an entire bloodline trying to escape a force that has been waiting for decades.

This evolution of the franchise's core theme makes *Bloodlines* feel fresh while staying true to what makes *Final Destination* terrifying. The fear of an unseen force manipulating the lives of an entire family adds a new layer of dread. It's not just about the next gruesome death—it's about the realization that no matter how far back this story goes, Death's grip has always been there.

By blending generational horror with *Final Destination's* signature death traps, *Bloodlines* ensures that the franchise's legacy—like its characters—can never truly escape fate.

Chapter 4

Tony Todd: A Horror Icon's Legacy

Few actors leave behind an imprint as chilling and enduring as Tony Todd. His deep, commanding voice and haunting presence have made him a staple in the horror genre for decades. While many fans first knew him as the terrifying Candyman, his role as William Bludworth in the *Final Destination* series cemented him as one of horror's greatest legends. Now, with *Final Destination: Bloodlines*, Todd makes his final appearance in the franchise, marking the end of an era.

Bludworth was never a traditional villain, yet his eerie knowledge of Death's design made him one of the most unsettling figures in the series. He wasn't just a mortician—he was a messenger, someone who understood the rules of fate in a way no one else did. His cryptic warnings, delivered in Todd's unmistakable voice, added a layer of mythology to the *Final Destination* films. While he never directly caused anyone's death, his ominous advice always left characters (and audiences) questioning whether he was truly an observer or something more.

Todd's presence in horror extends far beyond *Final Destination*. His breakout role in *Candyman* (1992) made him an icon. Unlike most slasher villains, Candyman was both terrifying and tragic—a vengeful spirit driven by love and injustice. Todd's portrayal gave the character depth, making him as compelling as he was frightening. His career also included roles in *Night of the Living Dead* (1990), *Hatchet* (2006), and countless other horror films and TV shows. No matter the project, his performances carried an intensity that few actors could match.

With his passing in November 2023, *Final Destination: Bloodlines* now serves as a fitting farewell to his legacy. The fact that his final film role is in the very franchise that helped define him for a new generation of horror fans adds a bittersweet weight to the movie. His return as Bludworth not only ties *Bloodlines* to the earlier films but also gives his character a sense of closure. For years, fans have speculated about who Bludworth really was—was he just a knowledgeable mortician, or was he Death's enforcer? *Bloodlines* may finally offer some answers.

Tony Todd's impact on horror is immeasurable. He was more than just a performer—he was a presence, a voice that could send chills down anyone's spine. With *Final Destination: Bloodlines*, audiences get to see him one last time, reminding us all why he was, and always will be, one of horror's greatest legends.

Chapter 5

The Anatomy of a Perfect Horror Death Scene

One of the biggest reasons *Final Destination* remains a horror staple is its ability to turn everyday situations into nightmares. The franchise's signature style isn't just about gruesome deaths—it's about the build-up, the tension, and the intricate chain reactions that make each kill feel terrifyingly plausible. With *Final Destination: Bloodlines*, the franchise pushes this formula even further, delivering what might be its most elaborate and shocking death sequences yet.

At the heart of every *Final Destination* death is one key element: inevitability. Audiences aren't wondering *if* someone will die; they're wondering *how*. This is what makes these movies so effective. Instead of relying on sudden jump scares, they stretch out the tension, forcing viewers to watch as tiny details—like a spilled drink, a loose screw, or a flickering light—slowly build toward catastrophe.

Take the now-infamous backyard barbecue scene from *Bloodlines*. It starts with something seemingly harmless—a piece of broken glass hidden in ice. But as the sequence unfolds, the tension mounts. A grill flares up unexpectedly. A trampoline tears at the worst possible moment. A garden hose whips around, knocking objects over. Every small detail escalates the danger until, in a horrifying instant, everything goes wrong at once. By the time it's over, the audience isn't just shocked by the brutality—they're left replaying the scene in their minds, analyzing every small misstep that led to disaster.

This meticulous approach to death scenes is what sets *Final Destination* apart from other horror franchises. In a slasher movie, the killer is the direct cause of a character's death. In *Final Destination*, the environment itself becomes the executioner. A seemingly harmless object—a tanning bed, an exercise machine, an escalator—suddenly becomes a death trap. These scenes work because they force viewers to engage with them. Every time a character walks into a room, audiences start scanning for danger. Is that power cord too close to the water? Is that candle burning too close to the curtain? The movies train viewers to anticipate the worst, making the final moment of impact feel all the more inevitable.

The best *Final Destination* deaths also tap into real-life fears. The highway crash in *Final Destination 2* made people afraid to drive behind logging trucks. The escalator scene in *The Final*

Destination made audiences second-guess stepping onto one. *Bloodlines* will likely do the same for backyard gatherings, turning what should be a normal summer tradition into something sinister.

With each new installment, the franchise has found new ways to terrify audiences, proving that when it comes to horror, there's nothing more effective than making the ordinary feel deadly. And in *Bloodlines*, Death is more creative—and cruel—than ever before.

Chapter 6

Horror's Future: What *Final Destination: Bloodlines* Means for the Genre

The horror genre is constantly evolving, shifting between trends that reflect societal fears, audience expectations, and technological advancements in filmmaking. In the past decade, we've seen the rise of psychological horror (*Hereditary*, *The Witch*), elevated horror (*Get Out*, *Midsommar*), and nostalgia-driven legacy sequels (*Halloween*, *Scream*). But *Final Destination: Bloodlines* reintroduces a type of horror that has been missing from mainstream cinema for years—one that thrives on tension, inevitability, and the cruel unpredictability of fate.

With *Bloodlines*, *Final Destination* proves that it still has a place in modern horror. The franchise never relied on supernatural creatures or traditional slashers. Instead, it capitalized on real-world fears—the idea that death is always waiting, and the most mundane moments can turn lethal. In a genre currently dominated by slow-burn storytelling and metaphor-heavy horror, *Final Destination* brings back the thrill of sheer spectacle, showing that audiences still crave creative, over-the-top, yet disturbingly plausible scares.

But what does *Bloodlines* mean for horror's future? For one, it signals a revival of high-concept horror franchises. Much like how *Scream* and *Halloween* successfully rebooted their legacies for new generations, *Final Destination* proves that well-executed sequels can breathe life into long-dormant properties. It also reinforces the demand for *event horror*—films designed to shock, entertain, and create lasting cultural impact. The success of *Bloodlines* could inspire other franchises (*Saw*, *Paranormal Activity*, *The Conjuring*) to take similar approaches, blending nostalgia with fresh storytelling.

Another significant aspect of *Bloodlines* is its generational horror theme. By expanding Death's reach beyond individuals to entire bloodlines, the film taps into a broader, more existential fear—one that aligns with the way modern horror has explored trauma, legacy, and fate (*It Follows*, *Talk to Me*). This suggests that the franchise could evolve further, finding new ways to expand its mythology beyond one-off disasters and into deeper, more layered storytelling.

On a technical level, *Bloodlines* also raises the bar for horror's visual spectacle. The *Final Destination* series has always been known for its elaborate,

Rube Goldberg-style death sequences, and with advancements in CGI and practical effects, *Bloodlines* delivers some of the most intense and meticulously crafted set pieces in horror history. This could influence upcoming horror films to invest more in dynamic, visually gripping sequences rather than relying solely on jump scares and minimalistic horror aesthetics.

Ultimately, *Final Destination: Bloodlines* isn't just a revival—it's a statement. It proves that horror doesn't have to choose between intelligence and entertainment. Sometimes, the best scares come not from abstract symbolism or psychological torment, but from the terrifying reality that Death is always waiting, watching, and—no matter how hard we try—impossible to escape.

Conclusion

Horror has always been about confronting our fears, but *Final Destination* takes it a step further—it forces us to acknowledge the one fear we can never outrun: death itself. Unlike slashers where the killer might be stopped or supernatural horror where the evil can be banished, *Final Destination* offers no escape. Death isn't personal. It isn't emotional. It's just waiting for its moment. And that's what makes the franchise so unsettling.

Since its debut in 2000, *Final Destination* has changed the way people look at the world. A simple road trip can feel dangerous. A routine visit to the dentist might make someone uneasy. A loose screw on a roller coaster could suddenly seem like a death sentence. The franchise's greatest power lies in how it turns everyday life into a potential horror scene, making us hyper-aware of the small details that could spiral into disaster.

With *Final Destination: Bloodlines*, the franchise evolves once again, proving that its core concept—cheating death—is just as terrifying as ever. By expanding the horror beyond individuals to an entire family line, the film deepens the story's sense of inevitability. Death isn't just coming for one group of people anymore—it's coming for generations. This shift in scope only reinforces what the franchise has always been about: no matter how much we try to avoid it, death catches up with us all.

But if *Final Destination* has one lasting lesson, it's this: fearing death won't stop it from happening. What we can control, however, is how we live in the meantime. The characters in the series are always running, always looking over their shoulders, but in the end, their fear changes nothing. The best horror movies don't just scare us; they make us reflect on our own lives. *Final Destination* reminds us that we never truly know when our time will be up—so what matters most is what we do while we're here.

As long as people fear the unknown, *Final Destination* will remain relevant. The franchise may take breaks, but Death never does. Whether *Bloodlines* marks the final chapter or the beginning of a new era, one thing is certain: Death isn't finished yet. And neither is our fear of it.